A Field Guide to the
FERNS AND LYCOPHYTES
OF LOUISIANA

A Field Guide to the
FERNS & LYCOPHYTES
OF LOUISIANA

INCLUDING
East Texas, Southern Arkansas, and Mississippi

Ray Neyland

Louisiana State University Press
Baton Rouge

Publication of this book is supported by DeeDee and Kevin P. Reilly, Sr.

Published by Louisiana State University Press
Copyright © 2011 by Louisiana State University Press
All rights reserved
Manufactured in Canada
LSU Press Paperback Original
First printing

DESIGNER: Michelle A. Neustrom
TYPEFACE: Adobe Caslon Pro
PRINTER AND BINDER: Friesens Corporation

All photographs are by the author. Drawings in the appendix are by Sisley Badolato.

LIBRARY OF CONGRESS CATALOGING-IN-PUBLICATION DATA

Neyland, Ray.
  A field guide to the ferns and lycophytes of Louisiana, including east
Texas, southern Arkansas, and Mississippi / Ray Neyland.
    p. cm.
  Includes bibliographical references and index.
  ISBN 978-0-8071-3785-7 (pbk. : alk. paper) 1. Ferns—Louisiana—Identification. 2. Ferns—
Texas—Identification. 3. Ferns—Arkansas—Identification. 4. Ferns—Mississippi—Identification.
5. Lycopodiaceae—Louisiana—Identification. 6. Lycopodiaceae—Texas—Identification. 7. Lyco-
podiaceae—Arkansas—Identification. 8. Lycopodiaceae—Mississippi—Identification. I. Title.
  QK523.N49 2011
  587.30976—dc22

                                                                    2010038288

To Margaret, the Muses, and the Marvelettes

CONTENTS

ACKNOWLEDGMENTS

Obtaining these images required considerable fieldwork where constant companions included alligators, snakes, mosquitoes, ticks, and red bugs. Repeated efforts were necessary to locate rare and elusive species. For their efforts in helping to locate these plants, I thank Richard and Jessie Johnson from Briarwood Nature Preserve, Garrie Landry from the University of Louisiana at Lafayette, and Christopher Reid from the Louisiana Heritage Program.

A Field Guide to the
FERNS AND LYCOPHYTES
OF LOUISIANA

INTRODUCTION

SCOPE AND PURPOSE OF THIS GUIDE

As a field guide, this book's main purpose is to assist the amateur botanist in identifying the recognized sixty-two species and two natural hybrids of ferns and lycophytes that are either native to or naturalized within Louisiana. Because most of these plants also grow in Mississippi, southern Arkansas, and eastern Texas, the guide is useful in those adjacent regions as well. This volume provides assistance at several levels. First, it features color photographs of individual plants in their natural habitat. Second, the guide describes each of the species in precise terms. Although a minimum of technical language is used, some standard botanical terms are beneficial in a field guide. Most of the terms are used repeatedly, and becoming familiar with their meaning will facilitate the task of identifying plants. A glossary and an appendix with illustrations of plant structures explain the botanical terms. Third, the guide offers dichotomous keys to aid the more serious student in making identifications. With a little practice, anyone can soon make good use of the keys.

PLANT DESCRIPTIONS

A brief description is given for each plant, including its basic features, its approximate size, its range within Louisiana and the United States, and any particularly distinguishing qualities. When relevant, other closely related species are mentioned to help avoid confusion in identification. In some cases, modern, traditional, and ethnobotanical uses of the plant are mentioned.

Plants are listed by family and scientific name in alphabetical order. Therefore, no phylogenetic treatment is implied. For each plant, the scientific name and a common name are given. The common names of plants may be useful and convenient in a local setting but may become confusing in a broader spectrum. For example, in the United States, *Equisetum hyemale* may be called either horsetail or scouring rush; in France, it is called prêle des prés; and in Germany, it is called Wiesen-Schachtelhalm. The advantage of using scientific names is that worldwide the same name is recognized for a particular plant, thus eliminating confusion concerning a plant's identity. The rules governing the scientific naming of plants are promulgated in the *International Code of Botanical Nomenclature.*

A plant's scientific name consists of two Latin or Latinized words followed by the author citation. The first word is called the generic name, and the second word is called the specific epithet. The author citation is attributed to the first person that described the species. Author citations are often abbreviated. The full names of these authors can be determined by referencing the book *Authors of Plant Names,* by R. K. Brummitt and C. E. Powell, or the web site of the International Plant Names Index (www.ipni.org). When the author's name is placed within parentheses and followed by a second name, this indicates that the second person has changed the original scientific name to the one shown. In some cases, distinguishable populations may occur within a species. If recognized by an author, subspecific names are made a part of the scientific name and placed after the specific epithet.

There are many directories to the common names of plants, and they vary as to the form used for any single plant name. Because there is no authoritative reference for common name forms, I have adopted my own standards in this guide. I have attempted to be consistent, usually favoring open or hyphenated compound terms over closed compounds, e.g., *lance-leaf* rather than *lanceleaf.*

GEOLOGIC HISTORY OF LOUISIANA AND ADJACENT AREAS

Louisiana and adjacent Mississippi, eastern Texas, and southern Arkansas lie completely within the geologic coastal plain. A dominant feature of the coastal plain is the Mississippi Embayment. It is a large floodplain that extends from the confluence of the Mississippi and Ohio rivers in southern Illinois to the Mississippi River Delta in southern Louisiana. The embayment is a rift in the North American continent that was formed in the Precambrian period (>543 million years ago [MYA]) as a result of tectonic forces and was subsequently filled with Precambrian- and Cambrian-period (495–543 MYA) sediments.

During the Cretaceous period (65–144 MYA), the area now occupied by the coastal plain was a shallow sea. In the early Tertiary period (starting about 65 MYA), the coastal plain began to form as a result of river and stream deposition into an ever-widening Gulf of Mexico and Atlantic Ocean. The Gulf of Mexico portion of the coastal plain was formed primarily by interior continental sediments from the Mississippi and Ohio rivers and by Rocky Mountain deposits from the Rio Grande, Missouri, Platte, and Pecos rivers.

Throughout the Pleistocene epoch (1.8–0.1 MYA), the coastal plain was repeatedly inundated during the warm interglacial periods. During these warm periods, the shoreline of Louisiana was as much as 58 km inland from its present position. During periods of glaciation when the climate was cool and dry, the shoreline extended considerably south of its present location.

Today, Louisiana, Mississippi, eastern Texas, and southern Arkansas are characterized as low and flat with high rainfall and warm temperatures. Major habitats include pinelands, savannas, river floodplains, swamps, marshes, and upland forests. Because the soil here is of marine origin, it is often sandy and acidic.

Most of the fern and lycophyte species of Louisiana and adjacent areas are well adapted to these environmental conditions. However, some species maintain a tenuous existence. For example, staghorn club moss makes only ephemeral appearances, apparently incapable of firmly establishing itself here. Another tropical species, the brown-hair lace fern, has managed to maintain a healthy but precarious colony in Terrebonne Parish, in southernmost Louisiana.

Some species typically found in more northern and therefore colder latitudes have also managed to push their respective ranges into the region. Examples include New York fern and maidenhair spleenwort. Thus, Louisiana's location accommodates a unique and broad assemblage of ferns, from common natives to rare immigrants. In the United States, Louisiana is second only to Florida in number of fern species.

The ancestors of land plants were probably green algae and originated in the ocean. The close relationship between green algae and vascular plants includes the shared presence of specific chlorophyll molecules, cellulose in cell walls, and starch within chloroplasts. Additionally, some green algae have the ability to form multicellular colonies as in the present-day *Volvox*.

Ancestral plants moving out of the water onto land would have faced the problems of drying out, adjusting to greater gravitational effects, and extracting oxygen from the air. The first nonalgal plants that arose were possibly the ancestors to the present-day bryophytes, which include the mosses, liverworts, and hornworts. Bryophytes are nonvascular, meaning they do not have xylem or phloem cells to transport dissolved nutrients and minerals to cells in the plant body. Additionally, bryophytes are like amphibians in that they are dependent on water for some stage of their life cycle. For example, they produce flagellated sperm that require a water film to traverse from male to female parts of the plant.

For plants to successfully colonize the land, several major developments occurred. One such development included the evolution of roots, which allowed plants to anchor themselves and to draw nutrients from the soil. Sugar-alcohol molecules called lignins became bonded to cellulose to produce stronger tissues to overcome increased gravitational effects. Openings in the plant tissue called stomata provided a direct interface to the air for oxygen and carbon dioxide exchange. Waxy secretions called cutin helped protect exposed tissue from desiccation. And vascular cells provided for the efficient delivery of dissolved nutrients and minerals within the plant body.

The first vascular plants arose about 450 million years ago in the Silurian period during the Paleozoic era. These plants, called psilopsids, of which the extinct *Cooksonia* is an example, probably produced spores. Extant spore-bearing plants with direct ancestors dating to this time include the ferns and lycophytes. Traditionally, the horsetails and the whisk ferns were included in their own respective divisions. However, recent molecular evidence suggests that these two groups are merely specialized ferns. During the Carboniferous period, about 350 MYA in the Paleozoic era, ferns and lycophytes occupied vast swamps and later became the major components of coal.

Composing the plant division known as Pteridophyta, the ferns, or pteridophytes, have a longer-known history than any other vascular plant division. They have a global distribution with approximately 7,000 species in 180 genera. Typically inhabiting cool and shady areas, they may be terrestrial, aquatic, epiphytic, or lithophytic. Ferns are herbaceous plants with either simple or compound leaves, called fronds, and they often produce a creeping rhizome. Plants that have only one kind of frond are called monomorphic; those that produce sterile fronds that differ in appearance from fertile fronds are called dimorphic. On the underside of the fronds are sporangia, which bear tiny spores and are usually clustered in a structure called a sorus. Sporangia are usually stalked and often exhibit an arc of specialized cells called an annulus, which releases the spores when they are mature. Most ferns are homosporous, meaning they produce only one type of spore. The fern families Marsileaceae, Salviniaceae, and Azollaceae are heterosporous, producing both male and female spores. Fern vegetative and fertile structures are illustrated in the appendix.

Another division of spore-bearing vascular plants, the Lycopodiophyta are often referred to collectively as lycophytes or as fern allies. This group comprises the three families Lycopodiaceae (club mosses), Selaginellaceae (spike mosses), and Isoëtaceae (quillworts). A fossil record that dates back to the Missisippian period (360 MYA) reveals that many species of the early lycophytes were large and tree-like. However, the approximately 1,100 species in existence today are considerably smaller. The lycophytes produce spore-bearing leaves called sporophylls. In the club mosses and spike mosses, the sporophylls are arranged in conelike structures called strobili. The quillworts produce sporophylls in a basal rosette. The club mosses are homosporous, and the spike mosses and quillworts are heterosporous. Lycopophyte fertile structures are illustrated in the appendix.

Both ferns and lycophytes have an alternation-of-generation life cycle that produces two different types of free-living—that is, two independent—forms. The most conspicuous form, called the sporophyte, has a full complement of chromosomes and produces spores. With half the amount of genetic material of the sporophyte, spores germinate to produce inconspicuous but free-living plants called gametophytes. These diminutive plants may be green and photosynthetic or nongreen and parasitic on fungi. Produced on the body of the gametophyte are structures called archegonia, which produce eggs, and antheridia, which produce sperm. Union of sperm and egg results in the germination of a new sporophyte plant, thus completing the life cycle.

SPECIES DESCRIPTIONS

AND PHOTOGRAPHS

Aspleniaceae

Asplenium platyneuron (L.) Britton, Sterns & Poggenb.

EBONY SPLEENWORT

From a short, creeping rhizome with fibrous roots, this perennial herb produces linear or oblanceolate 1-pinnate evergreen fronds. Up to 5 dm long, fertile fronds are longer and typically more erect than are sterile ones. Pinnae are oblong or quadrangular and glossy with small teeth; some exhibit a basal auricle. Petioles bear dark-brown or black scales throughout; the rachis is reddish or purple-brown and glabrous. Each sorus is linear with a white or translucent indusium. Ebony spleenwort inhabits mesic, often disturbed woods from eastern TX and throughout LA to southern WI and east to the Atlantic coastal states as far north as southern ME. Although mostly terrestrial, this species occasionally is epilithic. Plants are commonly grown in rock gardens and terraria.

Asplenium trichomanes L. ssp. *trichomanes*

MAIDENHAIR SPLEENWORT

This is an evergreen herb with a short, creeping, and often branching rhizome. The wiry petioles are red-brown or black-brown and glossy. The leaf blades are linear, up to 2 dm long, and 1-pinnate. Pinnae are oblong or elliptic with shallowly toothed or entire margins. Each sorus is linear with a translucent tan indusium. Sporulating in summer and fall, maidenhair spleenwort inhabits rocky crevices in Winn Parish in north-central LA and from eastern OK to central NC and north to Canada. Native Americans used the plant to treat cough, liver complaints, and female disorders.

Azollaceae

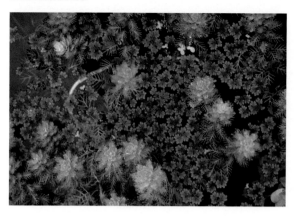

Azolla caroliniana Willd.

CAROLINA MOSQUITO FERN

A free-floating aquatic, this green or reddened annual herb produces a prostrate stem up to 1 cm long. The imbricately arranged leaves are alternate and sessile. Each leaf, up to 1 cm long, is two-lobed: the upper lobe is green and emergent; the lower lobe is floating or submergent and translucent. Heterosporous sporocarps are positioned at the base of lateral branches. Each megasporocarp produces a single spherical megaspore with a dark conical indusium. Each microsporocarp produces many microsporangia; microspores are beset with tangled arrow-shaped barbs. Rarely sporulating, Carolina mosquito fern inhabits ponds, swamps, marshes, and ditches in eastern TX and throughout LA north to MN and east to the Atlantic coastal states as far north as CN. The collective fronds often cover large areas and impart a red velvety texture to the water's surface. This species supplements its nutrition by capturing the nitrogen-fixing blue-green alga *Anabaena azollae* in cavities in its emergent leaves and stems.

Blechnaceae

Woodwardia areolata (L.) T. Moore

NETTED CHAIN FERN

From a creeping branching rhizome with brown lanceolate scales, this deciduous perennial herb produces dimorphic leaves. Up to 5.8 dm long, sterile leaves are pinnatifid with lanceolate lobes. Up to 7 dm long, fertile leaves are 1-pinnate with linear pinnae. The straw-colored petioles become red-brown near their base. Sori are linear-oblong and deeply sunken. Indusia are membranous and positioned under the sporangia. Sporulating from summer to fall, netted chain fern inhabits bogs, seeps, creek banks, and wet woods from western and southeastern LA to AR and eastern TX, and from MS to central FL and north to southern ME. Common on the coastal plain, this species is sometimes planted as a garden ornamental.

Woodwardia virginica (L.) Sm.

VIRGINIA CHAIN FERN

This is a deciduous perennial herb with a long, creeping rhizome and fibrous roots. Up to 1 m long, the 1-pinnate lanceolate leaves are widely spaced on the rhizome. Each petiole is black or purplish with dark-brown triangular scales. Pinnae are lanceolate and deeply pinnatifid. Sori are linear and situated along the costa and the costules in a chainlike pattern; indusia are elongated and membranous. Sporulating in spring and summer, Virginia chain fern inhabits swamps, marshes, ditches, and pond margins from eastern TX to western LA and from southeastern LA to FL and north to ME. This fern is used in wetland landscaping and as a garden groundcover.

Dennstaediaceae

Pteridium aquilinum (L.) Kuhn var. *pseudocaudatum* (Clute)
A. Heller

TAILED BRACKEN FERN

This is a colonial perennial herb with a branching, creeping rhizome. On a petiole up to 7 dm long, each deltoid or broadly ovate leaf blade is 2- or 3-pinnate and measures up to 8 dm long. The terminal segment of each pinnule is up to fifteen times longer than its width. The abaxial surface of each blade midrib and costa is either glabrous or sprinkled with soft hairs. Linear sori are arranged along the pinnules within false indusia formed by the revolute margins. Sporulating in summer, tailed bracken fern inhabits pine barrens and open woods throughout LA and much of the eastern United States as far north as MA. *P. aquilinum* var. *latiusculum* (Desv.) Underw., or eastern bracken fern, has pinnule segments that are no more than four times longer than wide; the leaf blade midribs and costae are shaggy. This variety inhabits open woods and pine barrens throughout LA and most of the eastern United States to southern Canada. Fronds of both varieties historically were used to stuff mattresses and burned to produce potash in the making of soap.

Dryopteridaceae

Athyrium filix-femina (L.) Roth var. *asplenioides* (Michx.) Farwell

SOUTHERN LADY FERN

This deciduous perennial herb produces a stout, short, creeping rhizome. Each petiole is straw-colored or reddish with a scaly dark-brown or black base. The 1-pinnate frond blades, up to 6 dm long, are ovate or lanceolate; the pinnae are usually stalked, and the pinnules are finely toothed. Sori are straight or hooked- or horseshoe-shaped; indusia are elongate with glandular or nonglandular hairs. Sporulating in summer, southern lady fern inhabits wet woods and swamps from southern IL and southern IN to eastern TX, and throughout LA to northern FL and north to MA. This species has been used in traditional medicine to reduce labor pains and to induce lactation.

Ctenitis submarginalis (Langsd. & Fisch.) Ching

BROWN-HAIR LACE FERN

This evergreen herb bears brown furlike linear scales on its thickened rhizome. The oblong or lanceolate leaf blades are 1-pinnate-pinnatifid and glabrous or pubescent with yellow glands. Pinnule margins are ciliate. Round sori are submarginal and arranged in a single row. Indusia are round to reniform and early deciduous, though brown-hair lace fern sporulates throughout the year. The species inhabits cypress swamps, hammocks, and spoil banks in Terrebonne Parish in southeastern LA and in central and southern FL. Native to the tropical West Indies and Central and South America, the plant is rare in LA and endangered in FL.

Cyrtomium falcatum (L.f.) C. Presl

JAPANESE NET-VEIN HOLLY FERN

From a stout erect rhizome, this perennial herb produces oblong or lanceolate pinnately compound evergreen leaves up to 1 m long. Scales along the base of the petiole are ovate and orange-brown. Glossy, leathery cordate pinnae are ovate or falcate with long tapering tips and irregularly toothed margins. Round sori are scattered throughout the abaxial pinnae surfaces. Brown and often with a black center, each indusium is peltate. Spores are brown with winged appendages. Introduced from eastern Asia, Japanese net-vein holly fern inhabits stone and brick walls, rocky woods, and mesic forests in scattered populations in northwestern, south-central, and southeastern LA and from FL to eastern SC. Popular as a garden ornamental and potted plant, this species has escaped cultivation and become naturalized in the Southeast.

Cyrtomium fortunei J. Sm. var. *fortunei*

ASIAN NET-VEIN HOLLY FERN

Introduced from eastern Asia, this is a naturalized evergreen perennial herb. Petioles are densely covered with brown ovate or lanceolate scales. The pinnately compound leaf blades, up to 9 dm long, are lanceolate or often falcate. The pinnae are dull green and papery with minutely toothed margins. Each round sorus bears a whitish indusium that is typically shed before the brown winged spores mature. Asian net-vein holly fern inhabits stone walls, clay banks, and ravines in southeastern LA and in scattered sites in GA and SC. In traditional Asian medicine, the rhizome is prepared as a decoction in the treatment of hookworms, tapeworms, influenza, and measles. In the Southeast, plants are grown as garden ornamentals.

Cystopteris protrusa (Weath.) Blasdell
LOWLAND BRITTLE FERN

The creeping rhizome of this deciduous herb bears tan ovate or lanceolate scales, yellowish hairs, and persistent petiole bases. Leaves are lanceolate or oblong and 1- or 2-pinnate. Up to 4.5 dm long, the early leaves are sterile; the later leaves are fertile and longer. Petioles are green or straw-colored with a few scales at the base. Sori are scattered on the adaxial surface of the fertile leaves. An ovate indusium arches over each round sorus. Sporulating from spring to summer, lowland brittle fern inhabits mesic woods, stream banks, and ravines from West Feliciana Parish in southeastern LA to southern MN and east through western NC to CT and southern NY. Native Americans prepared the plant as an infusion to treat chills. The species is well suited for rock gardens.

Diplazium lonchophyllum Kunze
LANCE-LEAF TWIN-SORUS FERN

The erect rhizome of this evergreen herb bears dark-brown ovate or lanceolate scales. The greenish or purplish petioles are hairy. Up to 3.6 dm, each leaf blade is lanceolate or deltoid and 1-pinnate-pinnatifid; the pinnae are distinctly lobed. Adjacent to each elongated sorus is a linear indusium. Lance-leaf twin-sorus fern inhabits wooded slopes and stream banks in the hardwood forests of Weeks Island and Cote Blanche salt domes, which are located in south LA's Iberia and St. Mary parishes, respectively. Found nowhere else in the United States, this species is also native to Mexico and Central and South America.

Diplazium pycnocarpon (Spreng.) Broun

GLADE FERN

The creeping rhizomes of this deciduous perennial produce brown lanceolate scales with entire margins. Up to 7.5 dm long, each leaf blade is 1-pinnate with greenish or straw-colored petioles. Pinnae are entire or shallowly toothed and sometimes auriculate at their base. Elongated sori are straight or falcate with laterally attached indusia. Glade fern inhabits mesic woods along slopes or ravines from West Feliciana and Iberia parishes in southern LA over to northern FL and north to Canada. This species is listed as either endangered or threatened in the northern part of its range. Practitioners of traditional medicine used the plant to treat lung and spleen ailments.

Dryopteris celsa (W. Palmer) Small
LOG FERN

From a creeping rhizome, this perennial herb produces 1-pinnate-pinnatifid ovate or lanceolate leaves up to 1.2 m long. The pinnae are linear, lanceolate, or oblong. The upper pinnae are fertile and similar to the lower pinnae, which are sterile. Densely arranged scales on the lower petiole often exhibit a darker central stripe. Each sorus is round with a reniform indusium. Sporulating in summer, log fern inhabits seeps, hammocks, and swamps from northern LA to southern MO and east to the Atlantic coastal states from NC to Long Island, NY. This natural fertile hybrid is derived from *D. ludoviciana* and *D. goldiana* (Hook. ex Goldie) Gray. Plants have been used in traditional medicine to expel tapeworms.

Dryopteris ludoviciana (Kunze) Small

SOUTHERN WOOD FERN

From a short creeping rhizome, this evergreen perennial herb produces 1-pinnate-pinnatifid monomorphic leaves up to 1.2 m long. The upper pinnae are fertile and distinctly narrower than the sterile pinnae below. Petioles bear conspicuous cinnamon-colored lanceolate or ovate scales. Each sorus is round with a reniform indusium. Southern wood fern inhabits wet woods and swamps in southeastern LA and from FL to central GA, eastern SC, and eastern NC. Plants have been used in traditional medicine to treat tapeworms. Where their ranges overlap, this species and *D. celsa* produce sterile hybrids.

Onoclea sensibilis L.

SENSITIVE FERN

From a creeping rhizome, this deciduous perennial herb produces dimorphic leaves. On a winged black petiole, each sterile leaf blade is yellowish green, deltoid, pinnatifid, and up to 3.4 dm long. The pinnae are lanceolate with entire or wavy margins. Fertile leaf blades, up to 1.7 dm long, are green and oblong with linear pennae. Pinnule margins are strongly revolute and appear beadlike. Bearing green spiny spores, the sori are enclosed within the pinnules. The indusia are deltoid and inconspicuous. Sporulating from summer to fall, sensitive fern inhabits swamps, marshes, and wet woods throughout much of the eastern half of the United States. The common name refers to the sterile fronds, which wither after the first frost. The fertile fronds persist through the winter and release their spores in spring.

Polystichum acrostichoides (Michx.) Schatt

CHRISTMAS FERN

From an erect rhizome, this perennial, dimorphic evergreen herb produces linear or lanceolate leaf blades on straw-colored and densely scaly petioles. Fronds are 1-pinnately compound; the pinnae are oblong or falcate with a prominent basal auricle and small spine-tipped teeth. The sori are densely arranged in the proximal pinnae; the indusia are peltate. Sporulating in spring, Christmas fern inhabits rich woods and rocky slopes in eastern TX and throughout LA, over to FL and north to Canada. The common name is derived from its evergreen nature. Native Americans used the plant to treat a variety of ailments, including rheumatism, pneumonia, and toothache.

Woodsia obtusa (Spreng.) Torr. ssp. *obtusa*
BLUNT-LOBED CLIFF FERN

The erect or horizontal short rhizome of this evergreen perennial bears brown lanceolate scales. Ovate, lanceolate, or rhombic leaf blades are 2-pinnate and up to 6 dm long. Pinnules are lobed and toothed and have glandular hairs. Petioles are tan or straw-colored. Round sori are positioned in a single row between each pinnule's midrib and margin. Scalelike indusia segments surround each sorus. Sporulating from summer to fall, blunt-lobed cliff fern inhabits cliffs and rocky slopes from eastern TX and the northern half of LA to northwestern FL and north to ME. This fern is especially suited for rock gardens.

Equisetaceae

Equisetum hyemale L. var. *affinae* (Engelm.) A.A. Eaton

HORSETAIL

From a creeping rhizome, this colonial perennial herb produces grooved, hollow, jointed evergreen stems, each up to 1.5 m tall. Each node bears a whorl of scalelike leaves that collectively form a sheath. Stems may be sterile or fertile; a brownish strobilus terminates each fertile stem. Arranged in whorls, the sporangiophores bear several sporangia each containing spherical spores. Strobili are present from spring to fall. Horsetail inhabits riverbanks, swamps, wet woods, and ditches throughout LA and most of the United States. Because of their high silica content, the stems are tough and abrasive. Early American settlers polished their pots and pans with the stems and called this species scouring rush.

Hymenophyllaceae

Trichomanes petersii Gray

DWARF BRISTLE FERN

This mat-forming epiphytic or epilithic evergreen has creeping threadlike stems that bear both glandular and rootlike hairs. Up to 2 cm long, the simple leaf blades are elliptic or oblanceolate with black branching hairs on their margins. A solitary sorus is produced in cup-shaped involucres near the leaf blade's tip. This mosslike plant also reproduces asexually from budlike structures formed on the fronds. Dwarf bristle fern occurs on rocks or at the bases of beech and magnolia trees in southeastern LA, southwestern MS, northwestern AR, and central FL, and from northern AL to southeastern TN and western NC. Easily overlooked, it is threatened in TN, AR, and NC.

Isoëtaceae

Isoëtes louisianensis Thieret

LOUISIANA QUILLWORT

This lycophyte is an evergreen perennial herb with a globose rhizome and brown roots. The spirally arranged bright-green leaves, up to 4 dm long, are linear with long tapering tips. Each sporophyll bears either a megasporangium or a microsporangium in a brown-streaked basal cavity. Maturing from winter to spring, megaspores are white with thick ridges. Louisiana quillwort is native to the state, inhabiting sluggish streams in Washington and St. Tammany parishes on the southeast border of LA. It has been proposed that this plant is a hybrid between *I. melanopoda* Gray & Durieu and *I. engelmannii* A. Braun.

Isoëtes melanopoda Gray & Durieu
BLACK-FOOTED QUILLWORT

This lycophyte is a deciduous terrestrial perennial herb with roots extending from the central groove of a two-lobed globose rhizome. It produces bright–green quill-shaped leaves up to 4 dm long. Each leaf is typically blackened toward its base. Each sporophyll bears either a microsporangium or megasporangium in a swollen basal cavity. Maturing in spring, microspores are gray and megaspores are white. Black-footed quillwort inhabits wet meadows, fields, and ditches from central TX through most of LA, excluding the coastal parishes, and north to SD, MO, and IL. Actively growing in winter and spring, these plants become dormant in summer.

Lycopodiaceae

Lycopodiella alopecuroides (L.) Cranfill

FOXTAIL CLUB MOSS

This lycophyte is an evergreen subshrub that produces creeping, ascending, and arching stems with small, regularly spaced adventitous roots. The densely arranged leaves are linear or lanceolate with toothed margins. Each strobilis is located on an erect stem up to 3 dm long and is somewhat bushy at maturity. Globose sporangia bearing granular-surfaced spores are located on the upper sporophyll surfaces. Sporulating from spring to summer, foxtail club moss inhabits wet savannas, bogs, and marshes in the southern two thirds of LA and adjacent TX, east to central FL, and north to southern CT. This and other members of the family have been used in traditional medicine to treat a vast array of ailments. *Palhinhaea cernua* (L.) Vasc. & Franco, or staghorn club moss, has a branching erect stem with nodding strobili. Found mostly in the tropics, this species inhabits wet pinelands and ditches on the outer coastal plain from eastern TX through the southern half of LA to central FL and north to SC. Within LA, plants appear briefly and may lack the ability to establish permanent populations.

Lycopodiella appressa (Chapm.) Cranfill
APPRESSED CLUB MOSS

This lycophyte is an evergreen subshrub with adventitious roots emerging from the underside of creeping horizontal aboveground stems. The densely arranged and appressed leaves have margins that are entire or bear a few scattered teeth. A plant may produce as many as 15 vertical stems, each up to 4 dm long, with leaves that are somewhat appressed and mostly entire. Sporophylls of each slender strobilus are ascending or slightly incurved with entire margins. Globose sporangia bear ridged spores. Sporulating in fall, appressed club moss inhabits wet savannas, bogs, and ditches from eastern TX to southern IL, throughout LA to FL, and north to Canada. This and other species of club moss are used in Christmas floral arrangements.

Lycopodiella prostrata (Harper) Cranfill.

FEATHER-STEM CLUB MOSS

This lycophyte is an evergreen subshrub with white, thickened adventitious roots emerging from creeping aboveground horizontal stems. The erect leaves on the horizontal stem have marginal teeth and are somewhat smaller than those attached laterally. Up to 3.5 dm long, each vertical stem produces somewhat appressed leaves with marginal teeth. Strobili are rather bushy with toothed sporophylls. Sporulating from spring to summer, feather-stem club moss inhabits wet pinelands, savannas, bogs, and ditches from eastern TX and southern LA to central FL, and north to eastern NC. This species has been reported to hybridize with both *L. appressa* and *L. alopecuroides.*

Pseudolycopodiella caroliniana (L.) Holub.

SLENDER CLUB MOSS

This lycophyte is an evergreen subshrub that has aboveground flattened horizontal stems tightly rooted to the soil. The leaves are lanceolate and arranged in two ranks along the stem. Leaves of the outer rank are laterally positioned and larger than those of the inner rank that stand almost erect. A slender vertical stem, up to 3 dm tall, bears linear or lanceolate bractlike leaves. Sporophylls of the strobilus are ovate or deltoid; sporangia are reniform, and the spores are wrinkled. Producing strobili in summer and fall, slender club moss inhabits wet pinelands, savannas, and bogs on the coastal plain from eastern TX and the southern two-thirds of LA to FL, and north to Long Island, NY. This species is endangered in NY and MD.

Lygodiaceae

Lygodium japonicum (Thunb.) Sw.

JAPANESE CLIMBING FERN

From a creeping, branching, hairy rhizome, this perennial herb produces vinelike fronds up to 30 m long. Leaf blades are 2-3 pinnately compound; the ultimate segments are lanceolate and lobed with pointed tips. Arranged in two rows, sporangia are produced along the margins of fertile pinnae, each covered by a false indusium. Spores are globose to somewhat deltoid. In LA, the species is evergreen, and sporulation may occur throughout the year. Introduced to the United States from eastern Asia, Japanese climbing fern has become invasive. It inhabits wet woods, ditches, and roadsides in eastern TX and southern AR and throughout LA to FL and north to NC. In traditional Asian medicine, a decoction of the dried leaves is used to treat coughs and urinary tract infections.

A FIELD GUIDE TO THE FERNS AND LYCOPHYTES OF LOUISIANA

Marsileaceae

Marsilea vestita Hook. & Grev.

HAIRY WATER CLOVER

This aquatic or semiaquatic perennial herb may form dense colonies, its roots arising from horizontal stem nodes. On sparsely pubescent petioles, leaves are floating or emergent. Blades are palmately divided into four glabrous or pubescent pinnae. Globose or elliptic sporocarps, each bearing two teeth, are produced on unbranched stalks near the petiole bases. Sporulating from spring to fall, hairy water clover inhabits pond edges and wet depressions throughout LA, north to Canada, and west to the Pacific coastal states. *M. macropoda* Engelm., big-foot water clover, is a nonnative species differentiated by its hairy petioles and branched sporocarp stalks. Inhabiting ditches, ponds, and marshes, this species occurs in southeastern LA, central and southern TX, southern AL, and northwestern FL. It and other species of water clover are popular aquarium plants.

Ophioglossaceae

Botrychium biternatum (Sav.) Underw.

SPARSE-LOBED GRAPE FERN

From a caudex, this perennial herb produces a solitary dark-green frond. The frond has a sterile trophophore and a fertile sporophore. The trophophore blade is 2- or 3-pinnate. The pinnules are lanceolate and finely toothed and remain green over winter. On a stalk up to 6 dm long, yellow sporangia are produced in two rows on 1- or 2-pinnately divided pinnae. Sporulating in late summer and fall, sparse-lobed grape fern inhabits wet and mesic woods in eastern TX, throughout LA to southern IL, and east to the Atlantic coastal states as far north as NJ. This and other species of grape fern are occasionally planted in woodland and shade gardens.

Botrychium dissectum Spreng.

CUT-LEAF GRAPE FERN

From fleshy fibrous roots, this perennial herb produces a glossy, leathery, 3- or 4-pinnate deltoid trophophore blade. Pinnules may be linear, lanceolate, ovate, or trowel-shaped with entire, toothed, or jagged margins. Emerging in spring, the green blades become somewhat bronzy during winter. Up to 4.5 dm long, the sporophore is 2- or 3-pinnate. Sporulating from fall to winter, cut-leaf grape fern inhabits various woods and meadows in eastern TX, throughout LA to southern IL, and east to the Atlantic coastal states as far north as Canada. Populations in LA and along the Gulf coast typically have trowel-shaped pinnules with toothed margins. Plants with deeply cut pinnule margins are more common northward.

Botrychium lunarioides (Michx.) Sw.

WINTER GRAPE FERN

The roots of this perennial herb are yellowish and somewhat fleshy. The one or two blades of the trophophore are 2- or 3-pinnate. Each pinnule is fan-shaped with a rounded tip and toothed margins. Up to 2 cm long, the stalk of the 2-pinnate sporophore is broadly flattened. Sporulating from late fall to winter, winter grape fern inhabits fields, prairies, roadsides, and closely cropped cultivated lawns in eastern TX, northern LA, and southeastern AR, and east to northwestern FL and north to NC. *B. jenmanii* Underw., or dixie grape fern, also has fan-shaped pinnules; however, its roots are blackish, and its sporophore stalk is only slightly flattened. This species inhabits various woods and lawns from Washington Parish in southeastern LA to northern FL and north to eastern KY and western VA.

Botrychium virginianum (L.) Sw.

RATTLESNAKE FERN

From a cluster of blackened cordlike roots, this perennial herb produces a solitary trophophore stalk up to 8 dm long. Each dull-green blade is lanceolate and 3- or 4- pinnate; the ultimate segments are linear with toothed margins and acute tips. The solitary sporophore is 2-pinnate and attached at the base of the trophophore blade. Sporulating in spring, rattlesnake fern inhabits open and shady woods throughout LA and most of the United States with the exception of the desert Southwest. Used by Native Americans for its properties as an emetic, diaphoretic, and expectorant, the plant was also a vital part of ceremonies to purge victims of the snake spirit.

Ophioglossum crotalophoroides Walt.

BULBOUS ADDER'S TONGUE

This deciduous perennial has a succulent cormlike rhizome and black hair-like roots. Emerging from the top of the rhizome are one or two leaves. Each pale-green trophophore blade is deltoid or cordate and lies nearly prostrate. Up to 1.5 dm tall, the sporophore bears up to eight pairs of linearly arrayed sporangia. Sporulating from late winter to early spring, bulbous adder's tongue inhabits secondary woods, fields, lawns, and ditches throughout LA and eastern TX to southern MO, and east to FL and north to southeastern NC. Most other members of the genus easily reproduce asexually via root buds, but this species typically does not.

Ophioglossum nudicaule L.
SLENDER ADDER'S TONGUE

From a short rhizome with yellowish or brown fleshy roots, this succulent perennial herb produces one to three fronds. Each frond is composed of an upright rachis that bears a sterile, ovate or elliptic, flattened dull-green blade with a pointed tip and a fertile stalked sporophore. Up to 2.7 dm long, the sporophore bears a pair of linearly arrayed sporangia. Sporulating from winter to spring, slender adder's tongue inhabits lawns, fields, and ditches in eastern TX, southeastern OK, southern AR, and throughout LA to FL and north to NC. *O. engelmanii* Prantl, or limestone adder's tongue, has a folded blade. Inhabiting fields, pastures, and lawns, this species ranges from TX and western LA to northeastern KS and southern MO, and east to central FL and north to northern VA.

Ophioglossum petiolatum Hook.

From an upright rhizome, this deciduous perennial typically produces fewer than eight dark-brown straight roots and from one to three leaves. Each trophophore blade is ovate and dull green with an acute tip. Up to 4.2 dm long, the sporophore bears as many as 30 pairs of sporangia. Sporulating from spring to early summer, stalked adder's tongue inhabits wet woods, ditches, and lawns in eastern TX, throughout LA to southeastern MO, and east to FL and north along the coastal plain to VA. Also found in Central and South America and Asia, this species may have been introduced into the United States.

Ophioglossum vulgatum L.

From an upright rhizome, this deciduous perennial produces up to 20 roots and a solitary leaf. The trophophore blade is ovate and glossy with a rounded tip. Up to 4 dm long, the sporophore bears as many as 40 pairs of sporangia. Sporulating from late winter to summer, southern adder's tongue inhabits secondary growth woods and forested bottomlands throughout LA and eastern TX to northwestern FL and north to southeastern MI, northern PA, and southern NJ. This species has been used in European traditional medicine to treat wounds, internal bleeding, vomiting, and snakebite.

Osmundaceae

Osmunda cinnamomea L.

CINNAMON FERN

This deciduous perennial herb is dimorphic and has a creeping woody rhizome with black fibrous roots. Leaves are 1-pinnate with deeply lobed pinnae. Sterile fronds may reach up to 1.5 m long; their petioles are covered with light-brown hairs. The succulent fertile frond is golden brown and withers soon after sporulation. Sporangia are neither clustered in sori nor enclosed by indusia. Spores are green. Sporulating in spring, cinnamon fern inhabits wet woods and seeps throughout most of LA and the eastern half of the United States. As part of the Native American diet, young unfurled fronds, now called fiddleheads, were boiled or roasted.

Osmunda regalis L. var. *spectabilis* (Willd.) Gray

ROYAL FERN

This perennial herb produces a stout trunklike rhizome with wiry black fibers. Leaves are bipinnate and dimorphic with winged petioles bearing light-brown hairs. The sterile leaves may reach up to 1 m long; pinnules are short-stalked with entire or remotely toothed margins. The lower portion of the fertile frond bears sterile pinnae; the upper portion bears shorter fertile pinnae. Sporangia are not clustered in sori; indusia are absent. Sporulating in spring and summer, royal fern inhabits swamps, bogs, stream banks, and pond edges in eastern TX and throughout LA to FL and north to Canada. Native Americans used the plant to treat a wide variety of ailments, including convulsions, insanity, and female disorders.

Parkeriaceae

Ceratopteris pteridoides (Hook.) Hiernon.

FLOATING ANTLER FERN

This aquatic herb is rooted or free-floating, and perennial or annual. Arranged in a basal rosette, leaves are dimorphic with inflated petioles. Up to 3.3 dm long, the sterile blades are deltoid or ovate and vary from simple to 2-4 pinnately or palmately lobed. Fertile leaves are 1-4 pinnate with the linear end segments. The sporangia are crowded between each segment's midvein and its revolute margin. Floating antler fern inhabits canals, bogs, swamps, marshes, lake edges, and ditches in southern LA and in central and south FL. Plants reproduce vegetatively from plantlets that bud from the sterile leaf margins. *C. thalictroides* (L.) Brongn., or water sprite, is usually rooted and its petioles are not inflated; each sporangia bears 32 spores. Inhabiting canals, bogs, swamps, marshes, and lake edges, this species occurs in southern FL and is rare in Terrebonne, Vermillion, and Cameron parishes in LA. Storm surges from Hurricanes Rita (2005) and Ike (2008) exerted negative pressure on the LA populations. *C. richardii* Brongn., or triangle water fern, bears only 16 spores per sporangium. It occurs in similar habitats in Livingston, Jefferson, and Orleans parishes in LA.

Polypoidiaceae

Pleopeltis polypodioides (L.) Andrews & Windham var. *michauxii* (Weath.) Andrews & Windham

RESURRECTION FERN

From small scaly rhizomes, this evergreen perennial herb produces long, creeping stems. Up to 2.5 dm long, each alternately arranged, 1-pinnately lobed leaf may be deltoid, elliptic, or oblong. The upper surfaces are glabrous and the lower ones are covered with copious brown round scales with transparent margins. Naked sori are clustered along the leaf margins; the spores are smooth with globose spots. Sporulating from summer to fall, resurrection fern is epiphytic on various hardwood tree species and epilithic on masonry buildings as well as sandstone and limestone outcrops throughout LA and the southeastern states as far north as VA. Curled and withered during dry weather, the leaves quickly become swollen when wet. With a decoction prepared from its fronds, Native Americans treated headache, thrush, and dizziness.

Psilotaceae

Psilotum nudum (L.) Beauv.

WHISK FERN

This is an epiphytic or terrestrial rhizomatous perennial herb with rootlike rhizoids. Up to 6 dm tall, the dichotomously branching stems are strongly ridged. Bractlike outgrowths called enations are awl-shaped. True leaves are absent. Yellow or green globose synangia are obscurely lobed and subtended by two-lipped outgrowths. Spores are reniform. Whisk fern inhabits swamps, hammocks, spoil banks, and rocky slopes from eastern TX and southern LA to FL and north to southeastern SC. Also found throughout much of the subtropical and tropical parts of the world, this species is sometimes used in traditional medicine. For example, its fronds supply an important ingredient in a Tahitian health tonic. Plants often become weedy pests in greenhouses.

Pteridaceae

Adiantum capillus-veneris L.

SOUTHERN MAIDENHAIR FERN

This deciduous herb has a short, branching rhizome that bears iridescent brown or yellowish scales. Up to 7.5 dm long, the leaves are arching or over-hanging. The 2-3 pinnate blades are lanceolate, ovate, or deltoid. Pinnules are fan-shaped or rhombic with lobed, finely toothed margins. Both petiole and rachis are dark purple or blackish. The submarginal sporangia are covered by oblong or falcate false indusia. Sporulating from spring to summer, south-ern maidenhair fern inhabits masonry walls and moist ledges in southwest-ern and southeastern LA and throughout much of the southern half of the United States. This species has been used in traditional medicine to treat a wide variety of ailments, including hepatitis, boils, and indigestion.

Adiantum pedatum L.

NORTHERN MAIDENHAIR FERN

This deciduous perennial herb has short, creeping rhizomes and fibrous roots. Up to 3 dm long, leaf blades are 1-9 pinnate and arranged in an overall fan shape. Pinnae are divided into segments that are straight on their proximal margins and sharply lobed on their distal margins. Each petiole is red-brown or black with bronzy scales near its base. Sori are produced submarginally and covered by a false indusium. Sporulating in summer, northern maidenhair fern inhabits rich deciduous woods from the eastern half of LA to central MS and from central OK to central SC and north to Canada. Native Americans used the plant to treat a variety of ailments, including rheumatism, fever, pneumonia, and asthma.

Cheilanthes lanosa (Michx.) D.C. Eaton

HAIRY LIP FERN

The short, creeping rhizome of this deciduous perennial bears linear or lanceolate brown scales. Up to 5 dm long, the leaves are 2-pinnate-pinnatifid with oblong or lanceolate blades. The basal pair of pinnae is shorter than the adjacent pair. Petiole and rachis are dark brown and hairy. The somewhat discontinuous sori are linear and protected by marginal false indusia. Sporulating from summer to fall, hairy lip fern inhabits rocky slopes and ledges from the northern half of LA and adjacent TX to MO, east to northwestern FL, and north to NY. To enhance water and nutrient uptake, the roots of this species host a symbiotic fungus.

Pteris multifida Poir.

SPIDER BRAKE

The short, creeping rhizomes of this evergreen perennial bear brown or reddish-brown scales. Up to 6 dm long, the oblong or lanceolate leaves are pedately divided proximally and 2-pinnately divided distally. The pinnae are lanceolate or linear. Margins of the fertile pinnae are entire; those of the sterile pinnae are irregularly toothed. Each rachis is winged. Narrow submarginal sori are protected by false indusia. Spider brake inhabits disturbed terrestrial sites and stone and masonry walls in the southern half of LA, eastern TX, east to northern FL, and north to NY. Introduced from Asia, it has escaped from cultivation and become naturalized within its range.

Pteris vittata L.

LADDER BRAKE

From a scaly creeping rhizome, this perennial herb produces a cluster of oblanceolate, 1-pinnate leaves. Each petiole and rachis bears scales and stiff, tawny hairs. Leaf blades typically do not exceed 5 dm long. The margins of the linear or lanceolate pinnae are involute and form false indusia; each uppermost pinna is elongated. Sporangia are tan with brown wartlike spores. From southern LA to FL and north to southeastern SC, ladder brake inhabits canal banks and masonry cracks in sidewalks, walls, and crypts. This naturalized introduction from Asia absorbs arsenic from the soil and stores it in its tissues. Recent studies show that it can be used to cleanse contaminated soil of this toxin.

Salviniaceae

Salvinia minima Baker
WATER SPANGLES

This naturalized aquatic perennial herb has a short, branching rhizome. The whorled, opposite, or alternately arranged floating fronds are each elliptic to nearly orbicular, somewhat spongy and up to 3 cm long. The lower surface is brown with slender, simple hairs; the upper surface is bright green with stiff, branched hairs at the tip. Submergent fronds are rootlike. Sporocarps are produced at the leaf's base and arranged in clusters. Those bearing microsporangia are distal to those bearing megasporangia. Sporulation is rare and occurs from winter to spring. Water spangles inhabits marshes, lake margins, and canals from southern LA to FL and north to southeastern AL and southern GA. Thought to have escaped from fishponds and aquaria, this native of Central and South America has become an invasive weed in much of its range. Studies show that it substantially displaces native vegetation.

Salvinia molesta Mitchell

KARIBA WEED

This introduced aquatic herb has horizontal rhizomes. Each floating frond is ovate or oblong, up to 4 cm long, and green with rows of stiff hairs. Each hair terminates in four parts that give it the appearance of an eggbeater. Submerged leaves are dark brown with rootlike fibers. The elliptic sporocarps form chains and rarely produce fertile spores. Kariba weed inhabits lakes, ponds, marshes, swamps, ditches, and sluggish rivers and streams from northwestern and southwestern LA to FL, and north to NC. Native to tropical America, this naturalized species has become a noxious weed in much of its range. Although sensitive to freezing temperatures and elevated salinity levels, the plant, under favorable conditions, displaces native species.

Selaginellaceae

Selaginella apoda (L.) Spring

MEADOW SPIKE MOSS

This lycophyte is a mat-forming perennial herb that produces sparingly branching, prostrate stems, each with small adventitious roots. Up to 2.25 mm long, the ovate or lanceolate leaves are dimorphic; one set is produced laterally along each stem, and another set is produced dorsally. Leaf margins are uniformly green. The lower portion of each ascending strobilus bears megasporangia, and the upper portion bears microsporangia. Meadow spike moss inhabits swamps, hammocks, ditches, and stream banks throughout LA and southeastern TX to southern IL, and east to the Atlantic coastal states as far north as southern ME. *S. ludoviciana* (A. Braun) A. Braun, or Gulf spike moss, has transparent leaf margins. Inhabiting swamps and stream banks, this species' range extends from southeastern LA to northern FL and southern GA. With their lacey, mosslike appearance, the plants are popular terrarium subjects.

Selaginella arenicola Underw. ssp. *riddellii* (Van Eselt.) R. Tyron
RIDDELL'S SPIKE MOSS

This lycophyte is an evergreen perennial herb with rhizomatous stems bearing scalelike leaves and tufts of adventitious roots. Up to 3 mm long, leaves along the aerial stems are deltoid or lanceolate with ciliated margins. Strobili are not conspicuously distinct from the aerial stems. Sporophylls are lanceolate or ovate; their bristly tips are often recurved. Riddell's spike moss inhabits rocky outcrops and gravelly or sandy soil from central and northwestern LA to central TX, north to northeastern OK, and from northern AL to northern and central GA. Of horticultural interest, this species is grown in rock gardens and as a potted plant.

Thelypteridaceae

Macrothelypteris torresiana (Gaudich.) Ching

SWORD FERN

This evergreen perennial herb produces a thick, creeping rhizome. Up to 1.5 m long, each 2-pinnate deltoid or ovate leaf bears silver-white hairs. Individual pinnules may be entire, pinnatifid, or toothed. Sori are round with minute and obsure indusia. Sword fern inhabits mesic woods and stream banks in southeastern TX and throughout LA to FL, and north to southwestern GA. Native to tropical and subtropical Asia and Africa, this species has become naturalized throughout the warm areas of the Americas. In Asia, plants are used in traditional medicine.

Phegopteris hexagonoptera (Michx.) Fée

BROAD BEECH FERN

This deciduous perennial herb has a long, creeping rhizome. Up to 3.3 dm long, each deltoid leaf blade is pinnatifid; the lower two pinnae are ascending and somewhat diverged. The petiole is straw-colored with basal scales, and the rachis is winged. Positioned near the pinnule margins, the round sori are naked. Sporulating in spring, broad beech fern inhabits mesic to wet woods, bogs, and stream banks in northern and southwestern LA and throughout much of the eastern United States. This fern is noted for the fragrant scent of its fronds and is occasionally used as an ornamental or ground cover in shade gardens.

Thelypteris dentata (Forssk.) E.P. St. John

DOWNY MAIDEN FERN

This evergreen perennial herb has a short, creeping rhizome and leaves up to 15 dm long. The base of each purple-brown petiole bears narrowly lanceolate, brownish hairy scales. On each 1-pinnately lobed blade, the tip is pinnatifid and the proximal pairs of pinnae are shorter. Sori are round with round-to-reniform tan hairy indusia. Downy maiden fern inhabits wet woods in the southern half of LA and from southern AL to FL. Native to subtropical and tropical Africa and Asia, it has become naturalized in the warmer regions of the Gulf coastal states.

A FIELD GUIDE TO THE FERNS AND LYCOPHYTES OF LOUISIANA

Thelypteris hispidula (Decne.) C.F. Reed var. *versicolor*
(R.P. St. John) Lellinger

HAIRY MAIDEN FERN

This evergreen herb has creeping or ascending rhizomes that tend to arch parallel to the ground. Straw-colored petioles bear hairy brown scales at their bases. Up to 5.5 dm long, leaf blades are 1-pinnately compound; the proximal pair of pinnae typically are shorter. Rachises and pinnae bear both glandular and nonglandular hair. Sori are round with round-to-reniform hairy indusia. Sporulating in spring and summer, hairy maiden fern inhabits wet woods, seeps, and stream banks in southeastern TX and across the southern two thirds of LA to FL and southwestern GA. This broad-ranging fern also occurs in Asia, Africa, Central and South America, and the West Indies.

Thelypteris interrupta (Willd.) K. Iwats.

WILLDENOW'S FERN

From a creeping cordlike rhizome, this perennial herb produces glossy ever-green leaves, each up to 15 dm long. Petioles are straw-colored and scaleless. The 1-pinnate glabrous leaves are somewhat deltoid and pinnatifid toward the tip; the basal pinnae are not diverged. The costae often bear ovate tan scales. Situated along the pinnule margins, sori are round with glabrous or hairy, round-to-reniform tan indusia. The abaxial leaf surface often bears red or orange glossy hemispheric glands. Willdenow's fern inhabits marshes, spoil banks, riverbanks, and ditches in St. Mary and Vermillion parishes in LA and in peninsular FL. Although rare in LA, this species is widely dis-tributed in tropical and temperate regions of Asia, Africa, Central and South America, and the West Indies.

Thelypteris kunthii (Desv.) Morton

SOUTHERN SHIELD FERN

From a creeping rhizome, this perennial herb produces ovate or lanceolate 1-pinnately compound leaves, each up to 1.5 m long. The petioles are straw-colored with linear or lanceolate dark-brown scales. Pinnae are oblong, deeply incised, and beset with stiff white hairs on the veins and blade. The proximal pinnae typically are not shorter. Each sorus is round with a round-to-reniform tan hairy indusium. Southern shield fern inhabits wet woods, swamps, stream banks, ditches, and roadsides in eastern TX, throughout LA to FL, and north to eastern SC. The Seminoles used the leaves to treat insanity and muscle weakness.

Thelypteris noveboracensis (L.) Nieuwl.

NEW YORK FERN

This deciduous perennial herb has a long, creeping rhizome. Petioles are straw-colored with tan or red-brown glabrous ovate scales. Up to 6.6 dm long, leaf blades are elliptic and deeply pinnatifid. The proximal several pairs of pinnae are distinctly shorter. Pinnule margins are entire or finely toothed. Sori are round with round-to-reniform hairy indusia. New York fern inhabits mesic woods, swamps, stream banks, and seeps from Washington Parish in southeastern LA to NC and north to Canada. Rare in LA, this fern becomes a common ground cover northward.

Thelypteris palustris Schott var. *pubescens* (Lawson) Fernald

MARSH FERN

This deciduous perennial herb has a long, slender, creeping rhizome. With blackened bases, petioles are straw-colored and may be glabrous or bear a few scales. Becoming pinnatifid near the tip, each 1-pinnate leaf blade is lanceolate and mostly glabrous at maturity and may extend up to 4 dm long. Pinnule veins resemble tuning forks. The length of the proximal pinnae is variable. The abaxial costae bear ovate tan scales. Sori are round with round-to-reniform hairy tan indusia and are located between the costule and pinnule margin. Sporulating in spring and summer, marsh fern inhabits swamps, bogs, marshes, riverbanks, and ditches in eastern TX, throughout LA to FL, and north to Canada. The Iroquois used the roots to treat a variety of gynecological ailments.

KEYS TO THE FERN AND

LYCOPHYTES OF LOUISIANA

Dichotomous keys are artificial in that they say nothing about how closely one plant is related to another plant. However, these keys provide a method whereby a particular plant can be identified. Dichotomous keys are designed as a series of paired, mutually exclusive statements that divide a set of plants into progressively smaller subsets until a single plant remains. Using keys takes some practice. But once the technique is mastered, the user can quickly identify ferns and lycophytes encountered in Louisiana and adjacent regions.

The first step in identifying a particular fern or lycoophyte featured in this field guide is to determine its genus. To do this, use the genera key. If this guide lists only one species in that genus, then the identification is complete. However, if two or more species are listed in the same genus, then use the appropriate species key to complete the identification.

Some of the morphological characteristics described in the keys will require magnification to observe. In such cases, the use of a simple ×10 hand lens or jeweler's loupe should supply the necessary magnification to make an accurate identification.

Distinguishing the several species of *Thelypteris* may prove to be particularly challenging. Members of this genus superficially look similar to each other. Paying close attention to the differentiating characteristics should ensure an accurate specific identification.

KEY TO THE GENERA

1. Plant floating free with leaves lying on the water surface   2
1. Plant otherwise   3
2. Emergent leaves green and spongy   *Salvinia*
2. Emergent leaves green or red; not spongy   *Azolla*
3. Plant floating free or rooted with leaves both lying on and extending well above the water surface   *Ceratopteris*
3. Plant otherwise   4
4. Leaf rachis elongated and vinelike   *Lygodium*
4. Leaf otherwise   5
5. Aerial stems hollow and jointed   *Equisetum*
5. Aerial stems absent, or if present, then not hollow   6
6. Leaves absent   *Psilotum*
6. Leaves present   7
7. Leaves quill-like and hollow   *Isoëtes*
7. Leaves otherwise   8
8. Sporangia arranged in a conelike strobilus   9
8. Sporangia arranged otherwise   12
9. Sterile leaves each with a ligule positioned near its base   *Selaginella*
9. Sterile leaves each without a ligule   10
10. Upright stems branching; strobili nodding   *Palhinhaea*
10. Upright stems not branching; strobili erect   11
11. Aerial stems with sparsely arranged scalelike leaves   *Pseudolycopodiella*
11. Aerial stems with numerous unmodified leaves   *Lycopodiella*
12. Plant epiphytic   13
12. Plant not epiphytic   14
13. Leaves entire   *Trichomanes*
13. Leaves lobed   *Pleopeltis*
14. Leaves divided into four cloverlike pinnae   *Marsilea*
14. Leaves otherwise   15
15. Leaves composed of a stalked cluster of sporangia arranged in two rows that arise at the base of or below a sterile leaflike blade   16
15. Leaves otherwise   17
16. Leaf blades compound   *Botrychium*

16. Leaf blades entire   *Ophioglossum*

17. Sporangia produced on either nongreen tissue or specialized stalks; rhizomes short, stout, and erect   *Osmunda*

17. Sporangia produced on green tissue; rhizomes typically creeping   18

18. Sori marginal and positioned under false indusial   19

18. Sori not positioned under false indusial   22

19. Rachis winged   *Pteridium*

19. Rachis not winged   20

20. Sporangia produced directly on separate and distinct leaf lobes   *Adiantum*

20. Sporangia produced otherwise   21

21. Petioles longitudinally ridged and grooved   *Pteris*

21. Petioles rounded   *Cheilanthes*

22. Sori elongate in a single row and immediately adjacent to the costae   *Woodwardia*

22. Sori otherwise   23

23. Sori elongate with linear indusium and positioned along veins   24

23. Sori round or elongate; if elongate, then without indusium   33

24. Sori generally along one side of vein only; rhizome scales latticelike   *Asplenium*

24. Sori often along one side of vein or curved around the end of the vein; rhizome scales not latticelike   25

25. Leaves dimorphic; fertile and sterile leaves strongly dissimilar in size and shape   *Onoclea*

25. Leaves monomorphic, or if dimorphic, then not strongly dissimilar   26

26. Indusia cup-shaped and composed of scalelike segments   *Woodsia*

26. Indusia absent, or if present, then otherwise   27

27. Veins in leaves forming areoles; each aerole with 1 to 3 included veinlets   *Cyrtomium*

27. Veins otherwise   28

28. Indusia attached at the center   *Polystichum*

28. Indusia attached laterally   29

29. Sori straight and elongate   *Diplazium*

29. Sori round   30

30. Upper costae rounded   *Ctenitis*

30. Upper costae grooved   31
31. Indusia attached at their narrow sinus   *Dryopteris*
31. Indusia, when present, laterally attached   32
32. Indusia absent   *Athyrium*
32. Indusia present   *Cystopteris*
33. Upper costae grooved   *Thelypteris*
33. Upper costae not grooved   34
34. Rachis winged   *Macrothelypteris*
34. Rachis not winged   *Phegopteris*

KEYS TO THE SPECIES

Adiantum
1. Pinnae of each leaf collectively arranged in a fan shape   *A. pedata*
1. Pinnae not arranged in a fan shape   *A. capillus-veneris*

Asplenium
1. Pinnae with conspicuous basal auricles that tend to overlap the rachis   *A. platyneuron*
1. Pinnae bases not overlapping the rachis   *A. trichomanes*

Botrychium
1. Sporophore stalk rises well above ground level; leaves absent in winter   *B. virginianum*
1. Sporophore stalk rises near ground level; leaves present in winter   2
2. Trophophore prostrate; leaves dying back in spring   *B. lunarioides*
2. Trophophore erect or ascending; leaves surviving through the season   3
3. Leaves gray-green and dull   *B. jenmanii*
3. Leaf blades green or blue-green   4
4. Leaves green in winter   *B. biternatum*
4. Leaves becoming bronze-colored in winter   *B. dissectum*

Ceratopteris
1. Sterile leaves with inflated petioles   *C. pteridoides*
1. Sterile leaf petioles not inflated   2
2. Each sporangium bearing 32 spores   *C. thalictroides*
2. Each sporangium bearing 16 spores   *C. richardii*

Cyrtomium
1. Pinnae leathery and glossy   *C. falcatum*
1. Pinnae papery and dull   *C. fortunei*

Diplazium
1. Pinnae with distinctly lobed margins   *D. lonchophyllum*
1. Pinnae with mostly entire margins   *D. pycnocarpon*

Dryopteris
1. Fertile pinnae narrower than the sterile pinnae   *D. ludoviciana*
1. Fertile pinnae same width as the sterile pinnae   *D. celsa*

Isoëtes
1. Leaf bases typically blackened   *I. melanapoda*
1. Leaf bases not blackened   *I. louisianensis*

Marsilea
1. Sporocarp stalks not branching; petioles sparsely pubescent
   M. vestita
1. Sporocarp stalks branching; petioles hairy   *M. macropoda*

Lycopodiella
1. Leaves on the horizontal stems typically with entire margins
   L. appressa
1. Leaves on the horizontal stems typically with toothed margins   2
2. Horizontal stems strongly arching   *L. alopecuroides*
2. Horizontal stems prostrate   *L. prostrata*

Ophioglossum
1. Stem rounded and cormlike   *O. crotalophoroides*
1. Stems not rounded   2
2. Trophophore veins forming concentric areoles   3
2. Trophophore veins not forming concentric areoles   4
3. Leaf blades folded along the midrib   *O. engelmanii*
3. Leaf blades not folded along the midrib   *O. nudicaule*
4. Tip of leaf blades rounded   *O. vulgatum*
4. Tip of leaf blades acute   *O. petiolatum*

Osmunda
1. Fertile leaves with monomorphic pinnae   *O. cinnamomea*
1. Fertile leaves with dimorphic pinnae   *O. regalis*

Pteris
1. Proximal portion of leaves pedately divided   *P. multifida*
1. Proximal portion of leaves not pedately divided   *P. vittata*

Salvinia

1. Each floating frond up to 3 cm long   *S. minima*
1. Each floating frond up to 4 cm long   *S. molesta*

Selaginella

1. Leaves on aerial stems not arranged in distinct ranks   *S. arenicola*
1. Leaves on aerial stems arranged in distinct ranks   2
2. Leaf margins transparent   *S. ludoviciana*
2. Leaf margins not transparent   *S. apoda*

Thelypteris

1. Leaf blades with all veins extending to the margin above each sinus
   2
1. Leaf blades with at least some veins not extending to the margin above each sinus   3
2. Proximal pinnae not greatly reduced   *T. palustris*
2. Proximal pinnae greatly reduced   *T. noveboracensis*
3. Veins of the ultimate leaf segments united below the sinus   4
3. Veins of the ultimate leaf segments not united below each sinus
   T. kunthii
4. Rhizome long-creeping; lower surface of costae with tan ovate scales
   T. interrupta
4. Rhizome short-creeping; lower surface of costae without tan ovate scales   5
5. Lower surface of costae with most hairs < 0.2 mm long; petioles purplish   *T. dentata*
5. Lower surface of costae with most hairs > 0.3mm long; petioles straw-colored   *T. hispidula*

Woodwardia

1. Leaves strongly dimorphic   *W. areolata*
1. Leaves monomorphic   *W. virginica*

APPENDIX

Illustrations of Plant Structures

FERN VEGETATIVE STRUCTURES

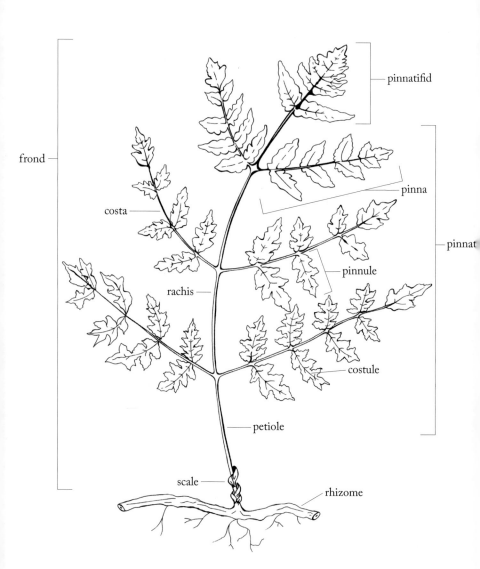

pinnatifid

frond

costa

pinna

pinnule

pinnat

rachis

costule

petiole

scale

rhizome

FERN FERTILE STRUCTURES

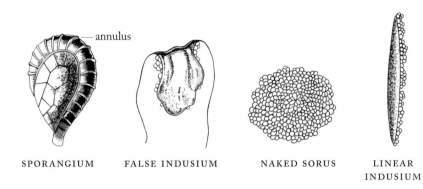

SPORANGIUM   FALSE INDUSIUM   NAKED SORUS   LINEAR
INDUSIUM

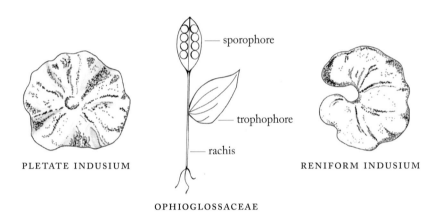

PLETATE INDUSIUM   RENIFORM INDUSIUM

OPHIOGLOSSACEAE

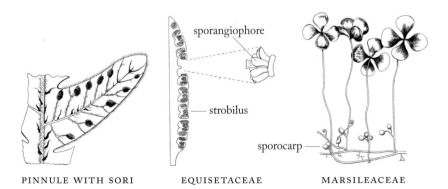

PINNULE WITH SORI   EQUISETACEAE   MARSILEACEAE

LYCOPHYTE FERTILE STRUCTURES

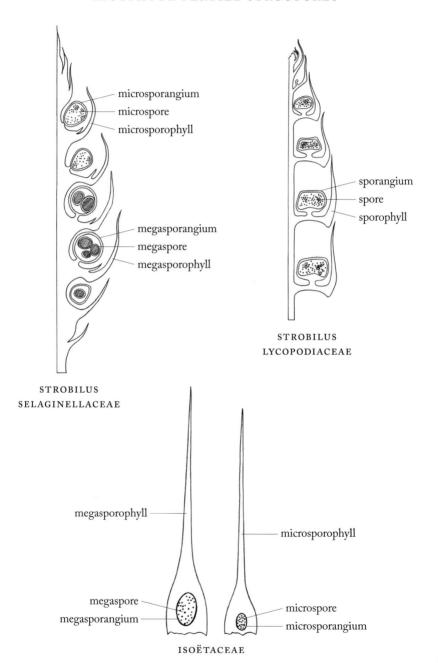

microsporangium
microspore
microsporophyll

sporangium
spore
sporophyll

megasporangium
megaspore
megasporophyll

STROBILUS
LYCOPODIACEAE

STROBILUS
SELAGINELLACEAE

megasporophyll

microsporophyll

megaspore
megasporangium

microspore
microsporangium

ISOËTACEAE

LEAF ARRANGEMENTS

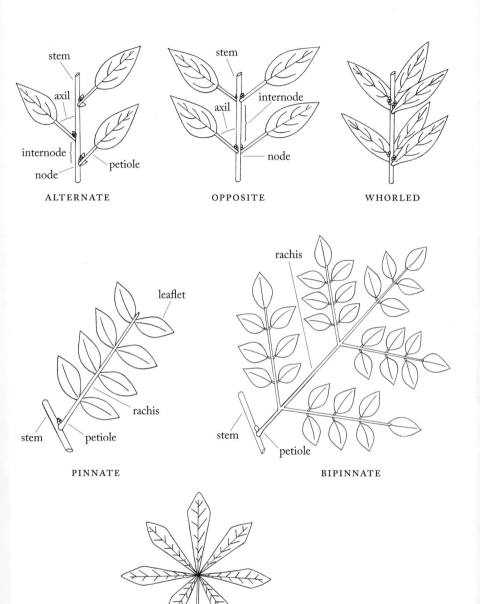

stem

axil

internode

node

petiole

ALTERNATE

stem

axil

internode

node

OPPOSITE

WHORLED

leaflet

rachis

stem

petiole

PINNATE

rachis

stem

petiole

BIPINNATE

PALMATE

GLOSSARY

The terms marked with an asterisk (*) are illustrated in the appendix.

Abaxial. Located on the underside of a structure such as a leaf.

Acute. Sharply pointed with an angle of less than 90°.

Adaxial. Located on the upper side of a structure such as a leaf.

Adventitious. Occurring in other than the usual location, such as roots appearing from a node.

Aerial. Existing or growing in the air rather than in the ground or in the water.

*Alternate. Only one leaf is attached to a single node.

*Annulus. An arrangement of thick-walled cells on the sporangium of ferns which ruptures to release spores when mature.

Antheridium. The male reproductive organ of spore-bearing plants (pl. antheridia).

Appressed. Lying flat against a surface.

Aquatic. Growing in water.

Archegonium. The female reproductive organ of spore-bearing plants (pl. archegonia).

Areole. A small space bounded by small veins.

Auricle. An ear-shaped part or appendage.

*Bipinnate. A pinnate leaf or frond that is twice divided; may be designated as 2-pinnate.

Bract. A modified, often smaller, leaf.

Caudex. The thickened base of an herbaceous perennial.

Cilia. Minute, short hairs.

Colonial. Having the tendency to grow in groups.

Compound leaf. A leaf with more than one leaflet per petiole.

Corm. A short, vertical, swollen underground stem.

Cordate. Having the shape of a heart.

***Costa.** The midrib of a leaf or pinna (pl. costae).

***Costule.** The midrib of a pinnule.

Creeping. Growing horizontally below ground, as in a rhizome.

Deciduous. Falling off or shed at a specific season or stage of growth.

Deltoid. Shaped like a triangle.

Dimorphic. Having dissimilar sterile and fertile fronds or pinnae.

Distal. Situated away from the point of attachment.

Disturbed. Changed from the natural state by humans.

Dorsal. The upper surface of a structure such as a leaf.

Elliptic. Shaped like an oval or ellipse.

Emergent. Projecting above the water's surface.

Entire. Having a smooth margin, as in a leaf.

Epilithic. A plant that grows on stone.

Epiphyte. A nonparasitic plant that grows upon another plant.

Falcate. Shaped like a sickle.

***False indusium.** A revolute leaf margin protecting the sporangia.

Fibrous root. A thin root arising from another root or from stem tissue.

***Frond.** The special name for a fern leaf.

Gametophyte. The haploid phase of a fern or lycophyte that produces gametes for sexual reproduction.

Glabrous. Without hairs.

Gland. Any structure that secretes a fluid.

Globose. Spherical.

Herb. Any plant that does not develop woody tissue.

Heterosporous. Producing two types of spores differing in size and gender.

Homosporous. Producing only one type of spore.

***Indusium.** A flap of tissue that covers the sorus in some ferns (pl. indusia).

Imbricate. Overlapping as in tiles on a roof or scales on a fish.

Involucre. A whorl of bracts.

Involute. A structure with the margins rolled upward, as in a leaf.

Lanceolate. Shaped like a lance.

Lateral. Situated at or along the side.

Ligule. A strap-shaped structure.

***Linear.** A narrow, elongated shape with parallel sides.

Lobed. Having deeply indented margins.

Lythophytic. Growing on stone or rocky soil.

Margin. An edge, as in a leaf.

*Megasporangium. A sporangium that produces megaspores.

*Megaspore. A spore that germinates to form a female gametophyte.

Megasporocarp. A sporocarp that produces female spores.

*Megasporophyll. A leaflike structure that bears megasporangia.

Mesic. A moderately moist habitat.

*Microsporangium. A sporangium that produces microspores.

*Microspore. A spore that germinates to form a male gametophyte.

Microsporocarp. A sporocarp that produces male spores.

*Microsporophyll. A leaflike structure that bears microsporangia.

Midrib. The central vein, as in a leaf.

Monomorphic. Having similar sterile and fertile fronds or pinnae.

Ob. Prefix indicating *the reverse of*, as in a leaf or bract (e.g. lanceolate, oblanceolate).

Oblong. An elongated shape with parallel sides.

*Opposite. Two leaves attached at the same node.

Orbicular. Circular in outline.

Ovate. Shaped like an egg.

*Palmate. Having three or more structures radiating from a central point.

Pedate. Having palmately divided lobes with the lobes cleft.

*Peltate. Having the stem or petiole attached to the lower surface rather than at the base or margin, as in a leaf or indusium.

Perennial. A plant that lives for more than two growing seasons.

*Petiole. The stalk of a leaf.

*Pinna. The primary division of a frond (pl. pinnae).

*Pinnate. A leaf with segments arranged on each side of the rachis like the veins in a feather; may be designated as 1-pinnate; further divisions are designated as 2-pinnate, 3-pinnate, etc.

*Pinnatifid. A leaf or frond that is pinnately divided or cleft deeply but not to the midrib.

*Pinnule. The ultimate division of a frond.

Prostrate. Positioned flat on the ground, as in a stem.

Proximal. Situated near the point of attachment.

Pubescent. Having hairs.

Quandrangular. Having four sides.

*Rachis. The main stem of a compound leaf (pl. rachises).

Remote. Separated by an interval or space greater than usual.

*Reniform. Shaped like a kidney.

Revolute. A structure with the margins rolled downward, as in a leaf.

Rhizoid. Rootlike filaments that absorb nutrients and water.

Rhizome. An underground stem that is typically horizontal.

Rhombic. Diamond-shaped.

*Scale. A small, thin, usually dry and often appressed structure.

Sessile. Directly attached, such as a leaf attached to a stem without a petiole.

Simple leaf. A leaf that is not subdivided into leaflets.

Sinus. The area between the lobes of a leaf.

*Sorus. A collection of sporangia (pl. sori).

*Sporangiophore. A stalked, peltate structure bearing sporangia in family Equisetaceae.

*Sporangium. The structure that gives rise to individual spores (pl. sporangia).

*Spore. The reproductive body of a fern or lycophyte sporophyte that germinates to produce a gametophyte.

*Sporocarp. A modified sorus enclosed by tissue in the families Azollaceae, Marsilleaceae, and Salviniaceae.

*Sporophore. A spore-bearing branch or organ.

*Sporophyll. A spore-bearing leaf or frond.

Sporophyte. The conspicuous form of a fern or lycophyte that produces spores.

Sporulation. The formation of spores.

*Strobilus. An aggregation of sporophylls resembling a cone (pl. strobili).

Submarginal. Adjacent to the margin.

Subshrub. A plant with herbaceous annual growth but with a woody base.

Subtend. To occupy a lower position.

Succulent. Having moist, fleshy tissue.

Synangium. A cluster of fused sporangia (pl. synangia).

Terminal. Situated at the end of a structure, as in a stem or leaf.

Terrestrial. Growing from land.

*Trophophore. The rachis and leaflike blade portion of the frond in family Ophioglossaceae.

Truncate. Having the end square or even.

Ultimate. The final division or segment in a series.

*Whorled. Three or more leaves symmetrically attached at the same node.

Winged. Resembling a bird wing in structure.

SELECTED REFERENCES

Bower, F. O. 1963. The ferns (filicales). Vols. 1, 2, 3. Today & Tomorrow's Book Agency, New Delhi, India.

Brummitt, R. K., and C. E. Powell. 2004. Authors of plant names. Royal Botanic Gardens, Kew, UK.

Correll, D. S., and M. C. Johnston. 1979. Manual of the vascular plants of Texas. University of Texas at Dallas, Richardson, TX.

Flora of North America Editorial Committee. 1993. Flora of North America north of Mexico. Vol. 2. Pteridophytes and gymnosperms. New York and Oxford.

Long, R. W., and O. Lakela. 1971. A flora of tropical Florida. University of Miami Press, Coral Gables, FL.

Radford, A. E., H. E. Ahles, and C. R. Bell. 1964. Manual of the vascular flora of the Carolinas. University of North Carolina Press, Chapel Hill, NC.

Small, J. K. 1938. Ferns of the Southeastern States. Hafner Publishing Company, New York, NY.

Thieret, J.W. 1981. Louisiana ferns and fern allies. Lafayette Natural History Museum. Lafayette, LA.

Thomas, R. D., and C. M. Allen. 1993. Atlas of the vascular flora of Louisiana. Volume 1: Ferns & fern allies, conifers & monocotyledons. Louisiana Department of Wildlife & Fisheries Natural Heritage Program, Baton Rouge, LA.

Spearing, D. 2007. Roadside geology of Louisiana. Mountain Press Publishing Co., Missoula, MT.

USDA, NRCS. 2006. The PLANTS Database (http://plants.usda.gov). National Plant Data Center, Baton Rouge, LA.

INDEX TO

FERNS AND LYCOPHYTES